NEWBURN DRIVE

Design by Mike Blanc

Signposts
on the Road *to*
Wellville

*Risking a Life of Scarcity to
Gain a Life of Abundance*

Journaling the Journey

with

Vanita Oelschlager

and several backseat drivers

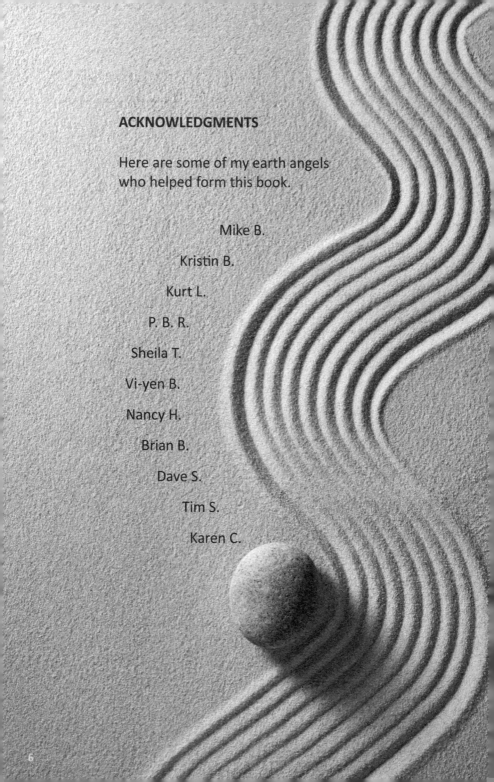

ACKNOWLEDGMENTS

Here are some of my earth angels who helped form this book.

Mike B.

Kristin B.

Kurt L.

P. B. R.

Sheila T.

Vi-yen B.

Nancy H.

Brian B.

Dave S.

Tim S.

Karen C.

Signposts on the Road to Wellville

Photography from 123rf® except pages 12, 14, 70 and 92 by David Shoenfelt, page 136 from iStock Photo®, pages 140 and 178 from Shutterstock® and page 152 from Google Art Project works in Gemäldegalerie, National Museums in Berlin.

Text by Vanita Oelschlager with noted contributors.

Design by Mike Blanc.

ISBN 978-1-938164-16-3

Published by **Newburn Drive**

For more information visit www.newburndrive.com

Printed in China

Friend,

The psalmist nailed it: a walk through the valley of death's shadow. When daylight feels like darkness, nightfall's like another scab torn away, and "Home" feels like too far to walk.

Maybe a walk through "the valley" is required in life; maybe not. Along my own pathway, the words you'll find here found their way to me. My work was to recognize and collect what was coming, trying to work its way in me. And I saved them like breadcrumbs, like signposts, I hope they'll be good travel companions and signposts for those times.

I could say this volume assembled itself over several years. I could say it worked on me, poking through my busy-ness.

I imagine you reading each page . . . thinking about it for minutes, days or weeks . . . then writing down what it means to you or makes you think about.

And so . . .

What am I doing here?

What are we doing here?

Truth lies ahead on the road.

Searching it out
is what makes
life real.

Tell the truth.

Seek the truth.

Recognize the truth.

You can't drink and dream.

And you must dream to live.

We do not have to wait for others to rescue us.
We are not victims.
There are no knights on white horses
waiting to rescue us.

Teachers may come our way,
but they will not rescue. They will teach.
People who care will come,
but they will not rescue.

Help will come,
but help is not rescuing.
We are our own rescuers.

Go ahead and say it – shout it even:

It HURTS!
I'm SAD!
I'm PISSED!
I'm LOST!
What's the use?

Then say it again.
And again.
And again and again.
OK. Now let's move on.

Recovery Lesson #1

It's not a "One and Done" thing.

Recovery Lesson #2

And neither is it a "One-Size-Fits-All" thing.

Recovery Lesson #3

It may not even be "Recovery" at all. Maybe it's rebirthing. Or repurposing. We are not here to say what IT is, how or why IT's done, or what's right for you.

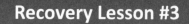

Only you get to say that.

"It is never too late to be what you might have been."

– George Eliot

If life goes crazy on you

do not do what you should.

Do only what you must.

Be flexible

Or be breakable.

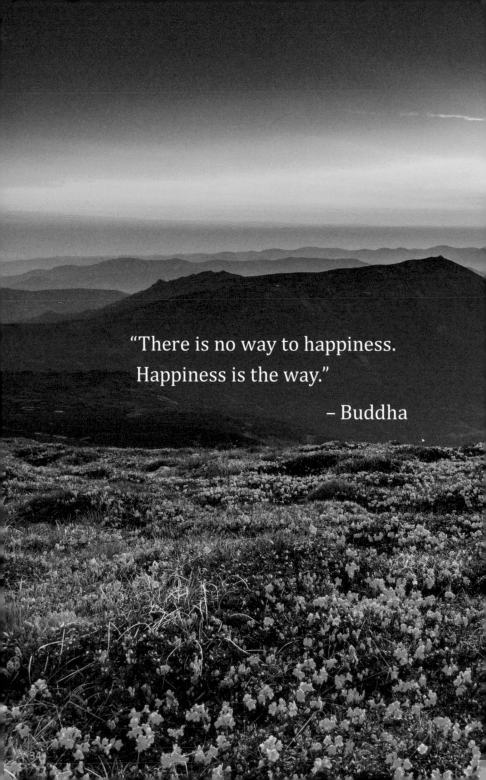

"There is no way to happiness.
Happiness is the way."

– Buddha

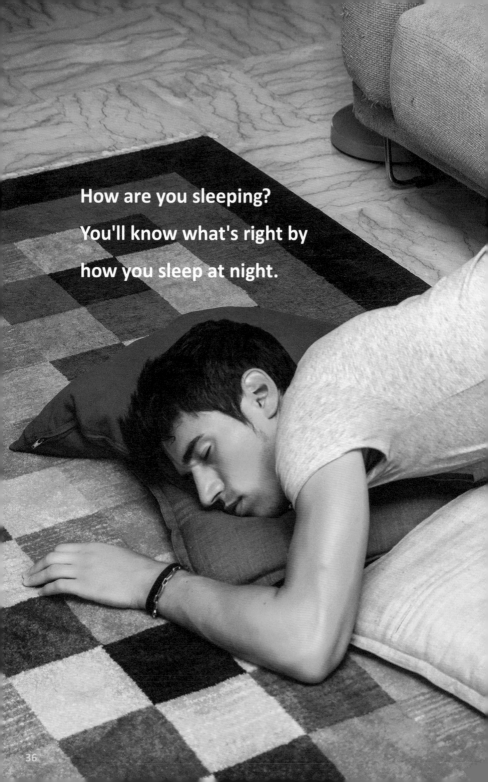

How are you sleeping?

You'll know what's right by

how you sleep at night.

Each day an assignment.
Each night a test.

You can't put off living
until you are ready.

The person you are
likes the person you are
when the person you are
is not drinking.

There is nothing you can
do that God can't forgive.

Without a body

we are still souls.

Without souls

we are nothing.

Spirit matters.

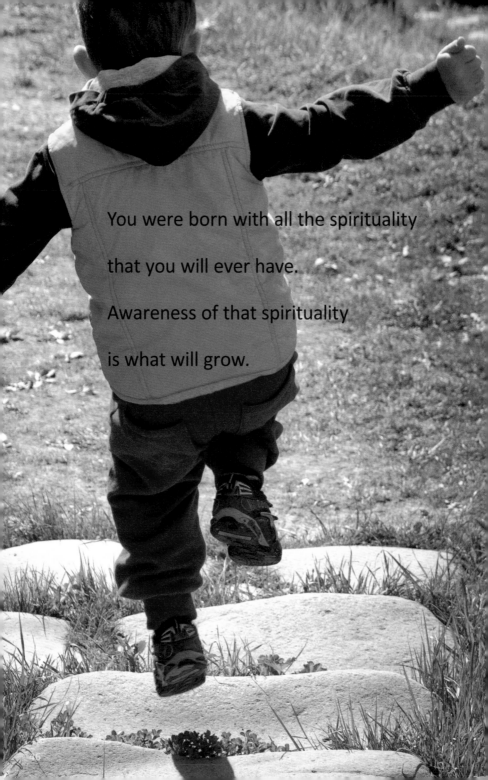

You were born with all the spirituality

that you will ever have.

Awareness of that spirituality

is what will grow.

Don't ever leave the
answers unquestioned!

H. A. L. T.

Stop and check
if you are too:

Hungry

Angry

Lonely

Tired

Be vigilant toward anyone
who is unsupportive–
or opposed to your pursuit
of being whole.

You have free will to change what you don't like.

Life weaves the patches,
You sew the quilt.

When things get bad,
scream with your head between two
pillows or while facing the ocean.

Quite liberating, actually.

Lord, help me to see myself.

Help me try to hear myself.

Help me try to help myself.

Help me try to become MYSELF!

You occupy sacred space.

When something wonderful
lands in your lap, don't stand up!

"I alone cannot change the world,
but I can cast a stone across the waters
to create many ripples."

– Mother Teresa

Everyone you encounter in life
was sent to teach you something.

You are headed where you have to go.

Where am I going?

"If you don't follow your dream, who will?"

– Emeril Lagasse

I think I know.
I THINK I know.
I think I KNOW.
I THINK I KNOW.

My mind is filled by it.
My dreams are full with it.
I have started this.
I am going to finish it!

Do it all …

Feel it all …

Write it all …

Share it all …

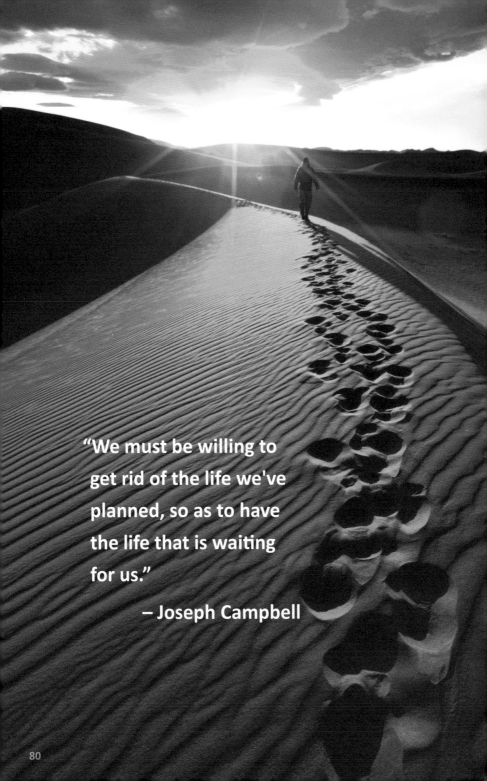

"We must be willing to get rid of the life we've planned, so as to have the life that is waiting for us."

— Joseph Campbell

What good is your sight
if you have no vision?

Walk to the edge...
Dare
Listen
Laugh

Love
Play
Learn...

This is it!

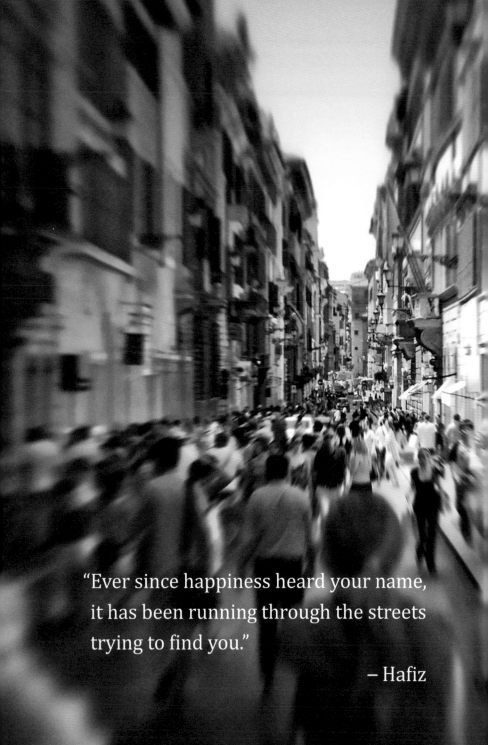

"Ever since happiness heard your name,
it has been running through the streets
trying to find you."

– Hafiz

Expect something marvelous . . . **Focus!**
And don't look away until you see it.

"There's no one alive
who is Youer than You."

– Dr. Seuss

There is a river that comes
from deep within.

Find that river.

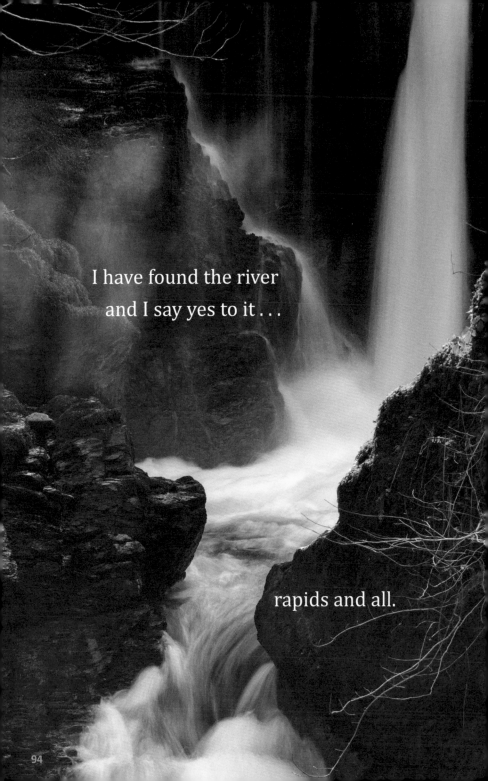

I have found the river
and I say yes to it . . .

rapids and all.

It is a marvelous thing to be in a ship
on a storm-tossed sea when one knows
that the ship will not sink.

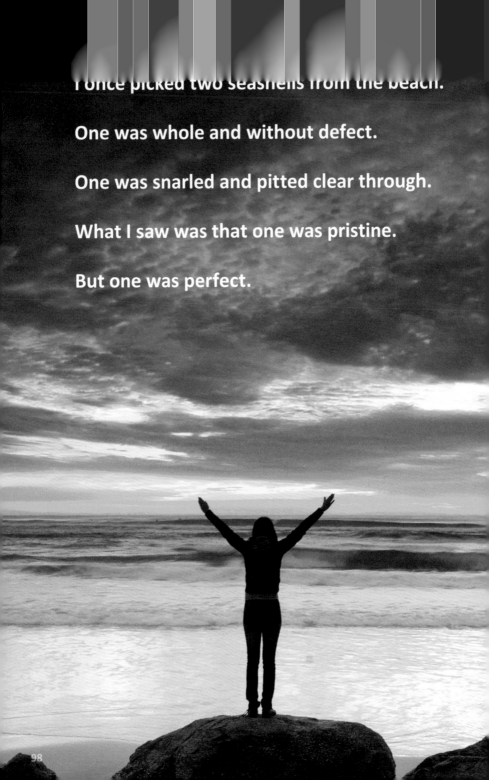

I once picked two seashells from the beach.

One was whole and without defect.

One was snarled and pitted clear through.

What I saw was that one was pristine.

But one was perfect.

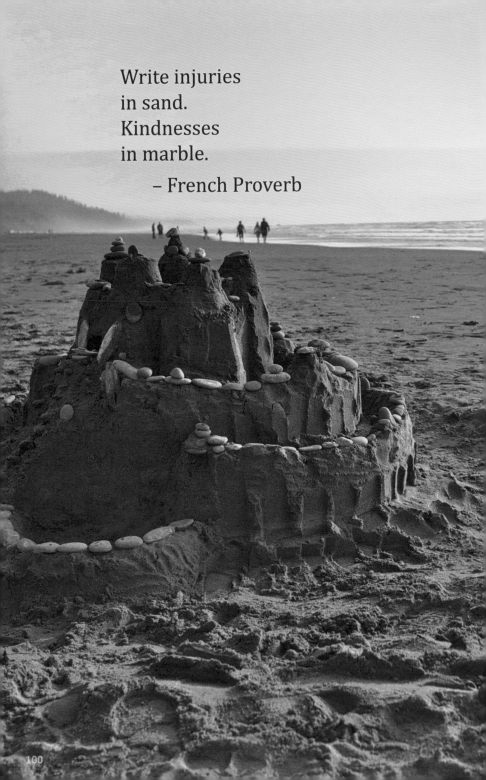

Write injuries
in sand.
Kindnesses
in marble.

– French Proverb

"The world is full of people who have never, since childhood, met an open doorway with an open mind."

– E.B. White

See enemy,
 See friend.

See maggot,
 See silkworm.

See doom,
 See grace.

Look with fear,
Or look with love.

You will teach others
What you have to learn.

"Here is a test to find if your
mission on earth is finished:
If you are alive, it isn't."

From *Illusions*

by Richard Bach

You are in your second blooming.

Don't play hard to get
when Joy is coming round.

You can't go home again
neither start over anew really
but you can continue and grow
new roots
new leaves
new seeing
new friends...

Although youth

may have passed,

childhood wonder

can live forever.

"Don't follow the path.
Go where there is no path
and start a trail."

— Ruby Bridges

"When your heart is in your dream,
no request is too extreme."

– Jiminy Cricket

If you're going to do this

you must do it for yourself.

In truth, you have only one life

with many ways to live,

so don't hold back.

Just Do It.

Don't let what you think you have learned get in the way of what you need to learn.

Find a spark catching flame
in a place away from the storm.

One step on the path leads to every next step. Pretty soon we look back and can see that we have been guided all the time.

"Wanderer, there is no path.
You lay a path in walking."

– Antonio Machado

I must follow my inner guidance.
When I <u>don't</u>
I feel a loss of energy,
great sadness
and spiritual deadness.

Today was the absolute worst day ever

And don't try to convince me that

There's something good in every day

Because, when you take a closer look,

This world is a pretty evil place.

Even if

Some goodness does shine through once in a while

Satisfaction and happiness don't last.

And it's not true that it's all in the mind and heart

Because true happiness can be obtained

Only if one's surroundings are good.

It's not true that good exists

And I'm sure you can agree that

The reality

Creates

My attitude

It's all beyond my control.

And you'll never in a million years hear me say that

Today was a good day.

Now read from the bottom to the top.

"I've heard that everyone wants to live on top of the mountain. But all the happiness and growth occurs while you're climbing it."

– Andy Rooney

What people think of me
is none of my business.

Decide who you are,
who you want to be,
and then do everything
in your power to be that.

"Stand for something or
you will fall for anything."

– Alexander Hamilton

I look at my life and discern the activities I repeatedly engage in that drain me.

I should dump it, delegate it,
or do it differently.

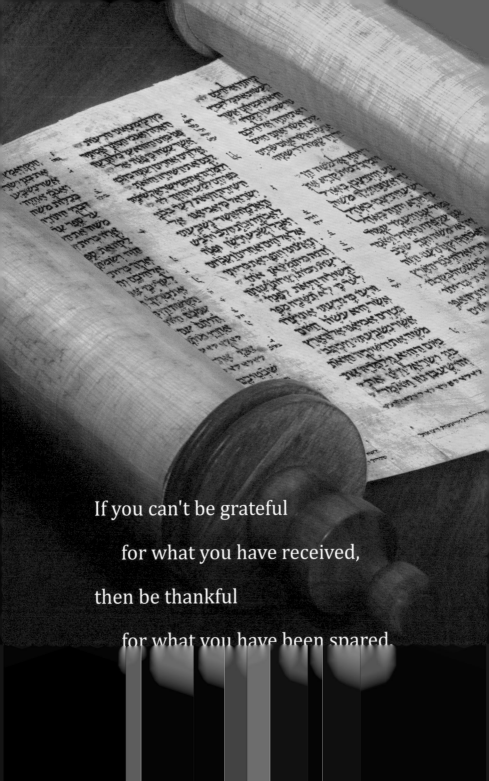

If you can't be grateful

for what you have received,

then be thankful

for what you have been spared.

"If what you have doesn't bring you happiness, how could you be happy with more?"

– Church Billboard

There is no instant gratification.
It is a daily process.

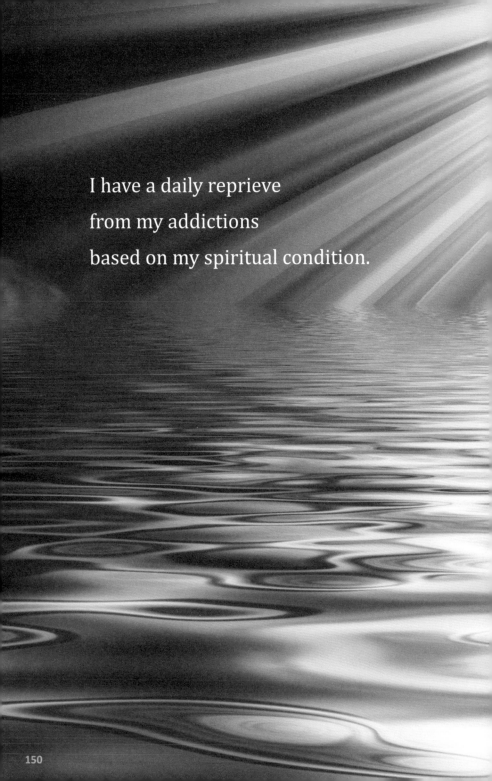

I have a daily reprieve
from my addictions
based on my spiritual condition.

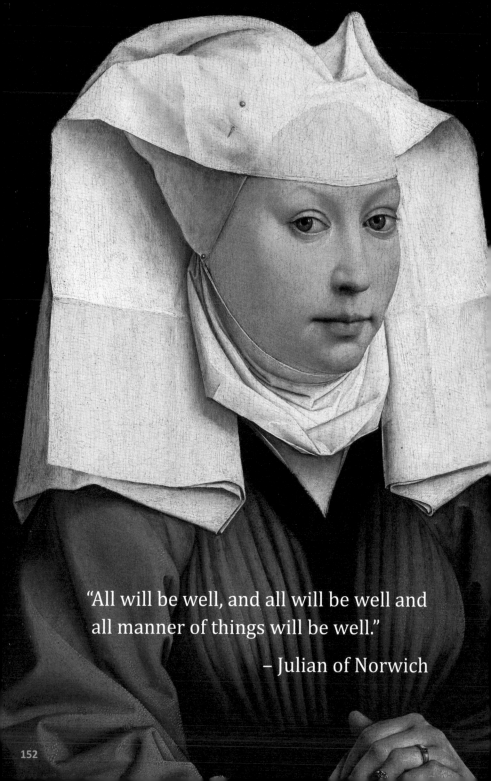

"All will be well, and all will be well and all manner of things will be well."

– Julian of Norwich

"Darkness cannot drive out darkness;
only light can do that.
Hate cannot drive out hate;
only love can do that."

– Martin Luther King, Jr.

Like an unseen fish
pulls the bobber,
an unseen God
tugs at your Heart.

"With each true friendship
   we build more firmly
   the foundation on which
   the peace of the whole world rests."

                        – Mahatma Gandhi

You're riding fast
right on the edge of life.

Slow down.

Whatever

overwhelms

you is trying

to get your

attention

to something

you're not

seeing.

. . . or doing.

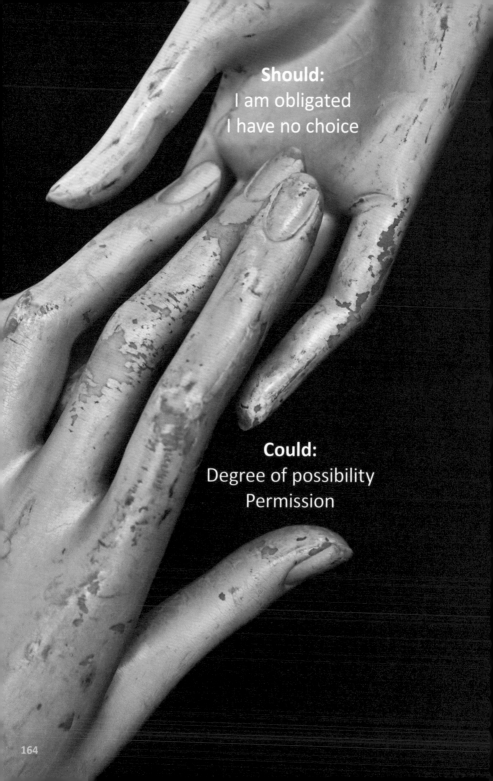

Should:
I am obligated
I have no choice

Could:
Degree of possibility
Permission

Only coulds
No shoulds

Be who you are,
not who you are told to be.

Your life is a fine instrument . . .

meant to be played lovingly.

Close your mouth.

Stop wracking your brain.

Trust in your higher power.

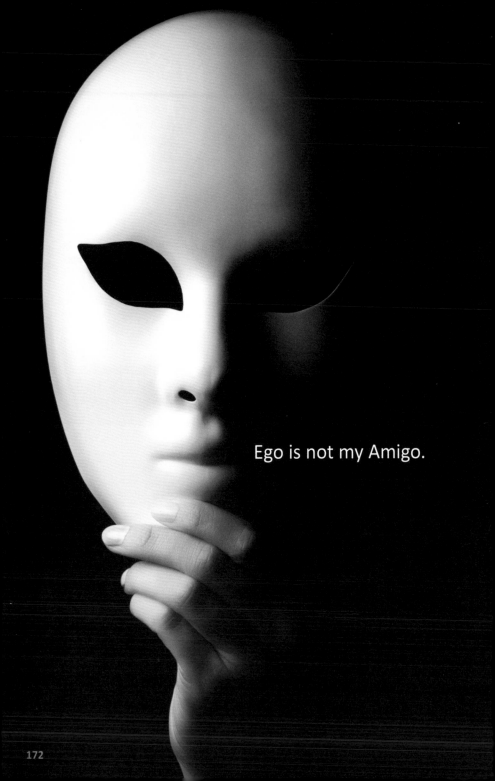

Ego is not my Amigo.

Forgive:

Fore – give

Give First

Return to your Mission Statement.

Or write a new one!

"We're all just walking each other home."

– Rumi

. . . here we are.

In my own life, alcohol sometimes became my best friend. Sometimes it was a power greater than myself that guided me.

Realizing this began my seemingly insurmountable dark night of the soul. I found an Anonymous group that gladly took me in; helped me through the part where feeling worse . . . meant I was making progress. All I had to do was follow some simple suggestions.

I am still on the path to wholeness.

The soul seems to thrive where personal growth is the primary value. The soul thrives more in small, local settings, where ambition is toned down by other values like those of family, place, nature and peace.

Let's all walk this path together. Life is about the path and our partners on it, not the destination.

Blessings to you,
Vanita